# Who Knew?! C      Facts About Animals that Live in the Serengeti

**Interesting things you never knew about wildlife in Africa, for kids and adults!**

Written by Lori Benson

© Copyright Lori Benson 2022 - All rights reserved.

The content contained within this book may not be reproduced, duplicated or transmitted without direct written permission from the author or the publisher.

Under no circumstances will any blame or legal responsibility be held against the publisher, or author, for any damages, reparation, or monetary loss due to the information contained within this book. Either directly or indirectly. You are responsible for your own choices, actions, and results.

Legal Notice:

This book is copyright protected. This book is only for personal use. You cannot amend, distribute, sell, use, quote or paraphrase any part, or the content within this book, without the consent of the author or publisher.

Disclaimer Notice:

Please note the information contained within this document is for educational and entertainment purposes only. All effort has been executed to present accurate, up-to-date, and reliable, complete information. No warranties of any kind are declared or implied. Readers acknowledge that the author is not engaging in the rendering of legal, financial, medical, or professional advice. The content within this book has been derived from various sources. Please consult a licensed professional before attempting any techniques outlined in this book.

By reading this document, the reader agrees that under no circumstances is the author responsible for any losses, direct or indirect, which are incurred as a result of the use of the information contained within this document, including, but not limited to, — errors, omissions, or inaccuracies.

## Animals listed in alphabetical order

Aardwolf

African Buffalo

African Elephant

Baboon

Bat Eared Fox

Bat faced Vervet monkey

Burchell's Zebra

Cheetah

Crocodile (Nile Crocodile)

Dwarf Mongoose

Eland

Giraffe

Grant's Gazelle

Grey Crowned Crane

Hartebeest (Coke's Hartebeest)

Hippopotamus

Hyena

Impala

Kirk's Dik Dik

Kori Bustard

Leopard

Leopard tortoise

Lion

Marabou Stork

Ostrich

Rock Hyrax

Secretary Bird

Southern Ground Hornbill

Superb Starling

Tawny eagle

Termites

Thomson's Gazelle

Topi

Warthog

Wildebeest

Index in the back

# Introduction

While this list is not all-inclusive, it is comprehensive and includes MANY of the animals that are seen in east Africa. I hope you enjoy this book!

When we went on safari in Tanzania, I was completely *amazed* at how many species of animals there are and how they each play a role in the ecosystem. There was so much I didn't know about the animals and how they lived.

It was fascinating to learn interesting things from our safari guide and from looking up information after we got home. Now, I've included some of this information in a booklet for you to enjoy!

*Lori*

# Aardwolf

- Did you know that the aardwolf is not related to aardvarks or wolves? It is the smallest of the hyena family.
- The aardwolf is nocturnal and spends the day underground sleeping in burrows.
- Like a cat, when the aardwolf needs to relieve itself, they use a specific area then they dig a hole, do their business, and then pile dirt on top to cover it up.
- The aardwolf has a long sticky tongue that it uses to insects and larvae.

**African Buffalo**

- There are 5 species of the African Buffalo. The Cape Buffalo can weigh as much as 2,000 pounds.
- Calves of the African Buffalo are only born during the rainy season.
- Cape Buffalo has 4 times the strength of an Ox.
- African buffalo is a large animal that can reach 6 to 11 feet in length, 5 feet in height, and weigh between 660 and 1900 pounds.
- African buffalo is well known for its exceptional memory. It will recognize a person (such as hunters) that hurt it in the past and it will attack it at their next encounter.

- Average lifespan of the African buffalo in the wild is 20 years.
- Due to their unpredictability, Cape Buffalo has been given the names of "The Black Death" and "widow maker" due to their aggressive nature.
- Cape Buffalo are found throughout Africa, but they tend to stay near a water supply and are usually found within 10 miles of a river.
- The African Buffalo is the only cattle that have not been domesticated.
- African Buffalo do not have very good eyesight but their hearing and especially their smell is exceptional.
- The African buffalo has a good relationship with many African birds such as the cattle egret or oxpecker. They are often found eating insects off the buffalo and will also warn the buffalo of approaching danger.

# African Elephant

- Elephants have around 150,000 muscle units in their trunk.
- Elephants have a dominant side. One tusk will often be shorter than the other and this is the one they use most often for digging. In the picture above, the left tusk is shorter and not as pointed as the right, this is the dominant side.
- Most of the elephants' communication is too low for human ears to pick up.
- Elephants DO have a better memory than people – in their brain, they have a larger temporal lobe than we do!
- Elephants have the largest brain of any land mammal, and they can weigh up to 5.4kg, compared to a human brain of 1.4g or 3lbs.

- A charging elephant can reach speeds of 40km/hr; compared to the average human of 9km/hr.
- The heart rate of an elephant is about 30 beats per minute while the average human heart rate is between 60 – 100.
- Elephants have 26 teeth, 12 of which are big flat molars about the size of a brick and can weight 4.5 lbs.
- Did you know that the only land mammal that can't jump is the elephant?

# Baboon (Olive Baboon)

- Baboons have existed for at least 2 million years. In 2015 a 2-million-year-old baboon fossil was found by researchers.
- When one baboon likes another and wants to be friends, they smack their lips.
- Baboons are very social and live in groups of around 50 but can also be as large as 200!
- A baby baboon is also called an infant!
- Baboons do not have prehensile (gripping) tails.

- Baboons share 91% DNA similarities with humans, this particular monkey is often argued to be an ape but is classified as a monkey.
- The lifespan of a baboon is about 30 years in the wild and up to 45 years in captivity.
- Unlike other monkeys, all baboons have long, dog-like muzzles, heavy, powerful jaws with sharp canine teeth.

**Bat Eared Fox**

- The favorite meal item for the bat eared fox are termites which makes up about 80% of their diet.

- Adult fox can have a head-body length of 55 cm and ears as long as 13 cm. Which is ¼ of their body length.

- A male fox is called a "dog," a female is called a "vixen" and a baby is called a "kit."

# Black-faced Vervet Monkeys

- The habitat of vervet monkeys is the savanna, coastal forests, and woodland environments with plenty of trees.
- The lifespan of the black-faced monkey is up to 30 years.
- The vervet monkey eats mostly fruit and leaves but will also eat insects, grubs, and sometimes rodents.
- The favorite place for the vervet monkey to sleep is over 20ft up in the trees.
- The vervet monkey's eyelids are lighter in color than the rest of their face, so they will raise and lower their eyebrows and flash their eyelids as a cautionary threat to others!
- Although very cute and small, the vervet monkeys do not make good pets! They are loud, messy, difficult to care for, and can be aggressive.

**Burchell's Zebra**

- Zebras live in family groups called harems.

- Zebra's sleep standing up so that they can quickly move if there is a predator.

- Burchell's Zebra, also known as the plains zebra, or common zebra, and is the only zebra that can be legally hunted.

- Zebras are smarter than wildebeests which is why the wildebeest like to travel with the zebras. They remember the way to go and do not get lost.

- A zebra can run as fast as 65 KM/H.

- Zebras will work together to look out for danger, which is why they often stand head to tail and rest their heads on the rumps of another. So that they can see predators coming from all sides plus the swooshing of the tail keeps the flies away.

**Cheetah**

- A cheetah's average life span lasts from 10-12 years.

- At full speed, the cheetah takes three strides a second, covering 7m per stride.

- The cheetah is not only the fastest land animal but did you know that a cheetah can go from zero to 60mph in three seconds flat.

- The name cheetah comes from a Hindi word, chita, meaning 'spotted one'.

- Cheetahs have evolved and adapted to live in an environment where water is scarce and can survive on drinking once every three to four days.

- A cheetah can have 2,000 – 3,000 spots!

- The Cheetah is the only big cat that can turn in mid-air while sprinting.

- Unfortunately, only 5% of cheetah cubs reach adulthood. This is due to other predators and diseases.

- A growl or chirp from a cheetah can be heard by the human ear as far as 2km away.

- Cheetahs have non-retractable claws, which keeps them from folding their claws to scale trees.

- On average, an adult cheetah needs about 2.8 kilograms, or 6 pounds, of meat per day.

## Crocodiles (Nile Crocodile)

- Crocodiles have the strongest bite in the animal kingdom. And the Nile crocodile is no different. Its bite can exert a force eight times more powerful than that of a great white shark and 15 times more than a Rottweiler's.

- The sex of crocodile hatchlings is determined by the temperature at which the eggs incubate. At 30°C or less they will be mostly female; at 31°C they will be mixed; and at 32°C, they will be mostly male.

- They are extremely dangerous! The Nile crocodile is very aggressive and has been known to attack people, unlike the American crocodile. About 200 people die every year from crocodile attacks.

- The Nile crocodile can grow to be as long as 4 – 5 m and weigh around 410 kg (900 lb).
- As its name, the Nile crocodile can be found in the Nile River which flows through 10 countries: Burundi, Congo, Egypt, Ethiopia, Kenya, Rwanda, South Sudan, Sudan, Tanzania, and Uganda.
- These animals are strategic hunters and can lie at the bottom, completely still, for up to 2 hours.
- Nile crocodiles have no natural predators. That means that everything else is prey!

**Dwarf Mongoose**

- The dwarf mongoose is the smallest carnivore in all of Africa, eating grasshoppers, beetles, and small lizards.

- Dwarf mongoose and hornbills work together at feeding time. They keep an eye out for each other and warn of any danger.

- The dwarf mongoose makes its home in old termite mounds which keep the internal temperature at a comfortable 31° C (87° F) during the summer.

# Eland

- The spiral in a common eland's horns looks a little bit like a unicorn's horn.

- Eland would make a good farm pet because the milk produced by common elands has double the amount of protein and about three times more milk fat than cow milk.

- The knees of an eland make clicking sounds when they walk.

- Did you know that the eland is the world's largest antelope? The eland looks like a blend between a deer and an ox. It is also the slowest antelope in the world.

**Giraffe**

- A newborn giraffe is still taller than most humans.

- A giraffe's neck is too short to reach the ground. To drink, giraffes first have to splay their forelegs and/or bend their knees, and only then can they lower their necks to reach the surface of the water.

- A giraffe heart weighs approximately 11 kilograms (almost 25 pounds) with an average resting heart rate of 40-90 beats per minute.

- The giraffe can run up to speeds of 35 mph, but only for a short while.

- The tongue of a giraffe can be up to 20 inches long and is blueish purple.

- Due to their height, the giraffe is considered one of the biggest pollinators due to their height and reaching flowers of the trees.

- Giraffes spend most of their day eating because they require over 75 pounds of food a day.

- The jugular veins of a giraffe contain a series of one-way valves that prevent excess blood flow to the brain when the giraffe lowers its head to drink.

- Giraffes don't have any upper front teeth. Most of their teeth are in the back for chewing leaves. They use their long tongue and lips to grasp leaves. Imagine not having front teeth!

- Giraffes have the largest heart of all mammals. The giraffe heart weighs 44 times more (and 5x the size) when compared to a human heart.

- The favorite food of the giraffe is the leaves of the Acacia tree.

- The thorns of the Acacia tree don't hurt the giraffe, and the leathery tongue resists the sharp thorns.

- Giraffes don't need much sleep, in fact, they get around 4 hours of sleep a day and it is often in very short intervals.

# Grant's Gazelle

- This species of gazelle resembles Thomson's gazelles but are noticeably larger and easily distinguished by the broad white patch on the rump that extends upward onto the back.

- Grant's live in herds ranging from 10 to 200 individuals depending upon the availability of food.

- Grant's can vary their body temperature in order to conserve water. Raising the body temperature during the day when it's the hottest causes the animal to sweat less, thus conserving water.

- Grant's gazelles are an important food source for many predators such as lions and hyenas.

- The Grant's gazelle stands 75–95 cm (30–37 in) tall.

- Grant's rely on leafy food to supplement water intake and have adapted to dry environments and can travel to semiarid areas where competition for food is not as great.

- Grant's are territorial and females are guarded by the dominant male. If a female tried to wander off too far it will be herded back by the male.

- Grant's Gazelle's are native to the countries of Ethiopia, Kenya, Somalia, Sudan, Tanzania, and Uganda

**Grey Crowned Crane**

- The grey crowned crane lives in wetlands like marshes, savannahs, rivers, and grasslands feeding on plants and insects.
- The grey crowned crane is a beautiful bird with a yellow crown of feathers on their head.
- On average, a grey crowned crane weighs around 7.5 lbs.
- The crane is nonmigratory and flies locally in search of food.
- The crane has a wingspan of up to 6 feet!

# Hartebeest (Coke's Hartebeest)

- The Coke's hartebeest is an antelope that looks a little like cattle with "lion-colored" coats, short horns, and a lump upon their neck. A juvenile is shown above.

- Hartebeest graze out in the open because they do not have a defense mechanism against predators. They are skittish.

- The hartebeest is usually found in small clusters of up to 20, but when migrating may join others and form a herd of over 100.

- Coke's hartebeest is the plainest and smallest subspecies, measuring 117 cm (46 inches) high and weighing 142 kg (312 pounds).

**Hippopotamus**

- The hippo's closest living relatives are whales and porpoises!

- In the wild, hippos can live to be about 40 years old.

- Although hippos can hold their breath for approximately seven minutes, most adult hippos resurface every three to five minutes to breathe.

- An average, full-grown male can reach up to 7,000 pounds; that's nearly the weight of a delivery truck!

- Hippos can't actually swim! They stand or push off from the bottom of rivers or ponds; their bones are too dense for them to float.

- A group of hippos is called a bloat.

- Hippos don't sweat blood. Hippo's skin secretes two substances that turn red (hipposudoric acid) and orange (norhipposudoric acid) and acts as sunscreens.

- Hippos are even more deadly than lions! Approximately 500 people are killed by hippos each year.

- Due to a meat shortage in the US, a bill was introduced House Resolution 23261 or "the American Hippo Bill" to import hippos to Louisiana. Fortunately, the bill did not pass.

- Hippos, native to Africa, were imported by Pablo Escobar and now there are over 100 hippos running wild in Columbia. Outside of Africa, Columbia is the only place that hippos can be found in the wild.

# Hyena

- There are three hyena species — spotted, brown, and striped. Spotted hyenas are the largest of the three.

- Female hyenas are very good mothers, investing more energy into their cubs than compared to other carnivores.

- Hyena cubs are born with black coloring and kind of resemble bear cubs (thus the name cub).

- The jaws of an adult hyena are very powerful (over 1,100psi) and can crush bones.

- Even though hyenas appear to resemble dogs, but, in fact, they are more genetically related to meerkats and mongooses! Hyenas have no relation to dogs.

- Hyena clans can be quite large (up to 100) but often they are found hunting in smaller packs.

- There is a common misconception that Hyenas are primarily scavengers. On the contrary, about 70-90 percent of their diet is composed of direct kills.

- Hyenas have many vocalizations with the best-known call being the hoot-laugh, or giggle, which has led humans to designate these animals as "laughing hyenas."

- Hyenas' "laughter" is actually a form of communication used to convey frustration, excitement, or fear.

- Female hyenas have three times as much testosterone in their bodies. As a result, spotted hyena societies are matriarchal. Girls rule!

# Impala

- In one single bound, an impala can leap as high as 10 feet and travel as far as 33 feet.
- Only the male impalas grow horns.
- Impalas are probably the most common and most commonly seen antelope in eastern Africa.
- They have a large tuft of black hair that covers a scent gland located above the heel on each hind leg.
- Impala produces barks-like sounds to alarm other members of the herd in the case of danger.
- The impala is an important prey species for several carnivores, such as cheetahs, leopards and lions.

- Like cattle, Impala are ruminants; they have four-chambered stomachs and at night they can be seen chewing cud.
- Male impalas are known as rams, while females are referred to as ewes.

# Kirk's Dik-dik

- The dik-dik is a dwarf antelope that stands 12 – 16 inches tall.
- The dik-dik earned its name from the sound it makes when it senses danger. It has an alarm call that sounds like "dik dik" by whistling through their noses.
- The dik-dik consumes enough water from the grasses and berries it eats that it does not need to drink water.
- Like a cow, the dik-dik has a 4-chambered stomach and chews its cud.

# Kori Bustard

- The Kori bustard is one of the world's heaviest flying birds. Weighing between 3 – 7 kg.

- The Kori bustard is often found with other game animals, feeding on insects disturbed by the larger animals.

- These birds spend most of their time on the ground, taking flight mostly to escape predators.

- Males produce a booming sound, inflate their necks, expose tail feathers and clap with their bills to attract females.

# Leopard

- Leopards are larger than a house cat, but leopards are the smallest members of the large cat category. They grow to only 3 to 6.2 feet (92 to 190 centimeters) long.

- Did you know there are black leopards? Black leopards have dark fur, which makes it difficult to see the spots. The spots are difficult to see, and they're commonly called black panthers.

- Adult leopards are solitary animals and only spend time with others to mate and raise their young.

- Pound for pound, the leopard is the strongest cat in Africa.

- The tail of a leopard is almost as long as its body!

- Leopards spend most of their time resting in trees and hunting at night. They have eyesight that is 7 times better than humans.

- Leopard cubs are born blind! When they open their eyes they are blue for the first few months.

- The leopard's spots are called rosettes because they look like roses.

- Leopards will eat almost anything; they are not picky eaters. To keep their food from being stolen by lions and hyenas, they will drag their prey up into trees to feed.

# Leopard Tortoise

- A leopard tortoise is an extremely slow animal, traveling at a maximum speed of 1 km/hour.

- The leopard tortoise is the only tortoise that can swim, in fact, they can also stay submerged for up to 10 minutes.

- The average length of a full-grown leopard tortoise is only 16 inches (40 cm).

# Lion

- Female lions, lionesses, are better hunters than male lions. Because of their smaller size, the female lions are 30% faster and have a more flexible body.

- After a kill, a male lion can eat over 90 pounds of food in one day!

- The Serengeti National Park has the highest concentration of African lions, at about 3,000!

- For a short distance, a lion can run up to a speed of 50 mph.

- Lions sleep a lot! Up to 20 hours a day is spent sleeping. They have few sweat glands so sleeping helps them conserve energy during the heat of the day.

- The phrase "King of the jungle" is incorrect because lions don't live in the jungle! Lions prefer the savannah because they prey on animals that live in grasslands.

- The manes of male lions are impressive. The manes grow up to 16cm long and are a sign of dominance. The older they get, the darker their manes get.

- Lion cubs are born with rosettes or spots that disappear as the cubs grow.

- A lion's roar can reach 114 decibels. Which is similar to a gas-powered lawnmower or a motorcycle.

- When a lion is born, it has a pink nose! As it ages, small, black spots appear. The spots keep getting larger until the nose is completely black, usually after 8 years. The lion in the photo is a young male.

# Marabou Stork

- The marabou stork is considered to be one of the ugliest animals on the planet.

- The stork stands up to 60 inches tall and weighs as much as 20 lbs.

- The marabou is a meat lover, a carnivore, who feasts on the carcasses and scraps of dead animals similar to vultures.

- The average lifespan for a marabou stork in the wild is 25 years.

**Ostrich**

- Ostriches are the world's largest bird, growing up to 9 feet tall and weighing about 330 lbs.

- An ostrich can run at sustained speeds of about 31 miles per hour.

- Ostrich eggs are also the largest. The eggs have a diameter of about 6 inches and weigh up to 3 pounds. That is 20 times the size of a chicken egg.

- An ostrich can reach a speed of 70km/h, and each stride of an ostrich can be as long as 5 meters.

- Ostriches have three stomachs because they need to metabolize the tough plant matter that they eat, which they can't do in just a single stomach.

- Ostriches have a long lifespan and live up to 30-50 years.

- A male ostrich is black and white (as in the photo above) while a female ostrich has brownish-grey feathers.

- Ostriches use their wings as rudders to change directions while running.

- Ostriches are omnivores, they like roots, seeds, and leaves but will also eat locusts, lizards and snakes.

# Rhinoceroses

- More than 40 southern white rhinos have been born in the Serengeti National Park.
- Nine critically endangered black rhinos (photo above) were relocated to the Serengeti in 2019 where the herd is slowly growing.
- The total rhino population in the Serengeti is approximately 160 animals.
- Black and white rhinos are actually – grey! The word "white" actually came from the African word "wide" and refers to its mouth size.
- Female rhinos are more sociable than the males.
- A group of rhinos is called a "crash".
- A rhino will poo about 26kg or 50 pounds in a single day!

# Rock Hyrax

- The rock hyrax looks like a very large guinea pig, but it is not a rodent.
- They like to sunbathe; the rock hyrax spends up to 95% of its day resting and lying in the sun.
- The rock hyrax has at least 21 vocalizations and lives in colonies of up to 80 individuals.
- Their closest genetic relative to the rock hyrax – in terms of species – is the elephant.
- The rock hyrax is an omnivore and feed on grasses, fruits, lizards, and scout around trash cans if the opportunity arises.

## Secretary Bird

- The secretary bird is an interesting bird as it looks like it has an eagle-like body and legs like a stork.

- The secretary bird has the longest legs of any bird of prey.

- Unlike most birds of prey, the secretary bird is largely land-dwelling, hunting its prey on foot rather than from the air; even though it is a good flier.

- Secretary birds use the thickened soles of their feet to stomp on their prey, stunning it and then swallowing it whole.

- Secretary birds can reach 4 to 5 feet in height and between 5 to 9 ½ pounds.

- How did the secretary bird get its name? One theory is that the feathers jutting out behind the bird's head reminded 19th-century Europeans of the quill pens that secretaries used.

- Secretary birds are carnivores (meat-eaters). Their primary diet consists of insects, rodents, lizards, and snakes.

## Southern Ground Hornbill

- The southern ground hornbill reproductive cycle is very slow, only producing two chicks every nine years, and usually only one survives.
- The hornbill is a very large bird weighing 4.9-13.7 lb (2.2-6.2 kg). Like a small turkey.
- The southern ground hornbill is endangered with an estimated total of less than 1,500 birds in the world.

# Superb Starling

- The superb starling is small but makes up for it with brilliant plumage of deep metallic blues, greens & chestnuts with bright white accents on the chest and underwing.
- Starlings often make their nests in acacia trees, anywhere from 5 to 20 ft from the ground.
- The Superb Starling is an omnivorous bird, feeding on insects and a variety of fruit and berries.
- Starlings are a plentiful bird and commonly seen throughout East Africa.

# Tawny Eagle

- This is a large eagle -- about 62—72 cm in length with a wingspan of 165-185 cm (64-75inches).
- These eagles are monogamous, they mate and pair for the life of the birds. Laying eggs annually between April to July
- One interesting characteristic that makes this eagle unique is that it prefers live prey.

# Termites

- There are over 2,600 species of termites worldwide and they are closely related to the cockroach.
- Termite mounds can be enormous with large ones over 30m in diameter.
- The termite mound is an extensive system of tunnels and conduits that serves as a ventilation system for the underground nest.
- Other animals will stand on the top of the termite mounds to use them to see in the distance or to reach tree limbs up above.

- Termites are blind and may die if exposed to the sunlight for any length of time.

## Thomson's Gazelle

- Did you know that all gazelles are antelopes, but not all antelopes are gazelles?
- Thomson's gazelle is a small gazelle, it stands from 55 to 82 cm (22 to 32 in) at the shoulder.
- Thomson's gazelle is among the most common antelope in the Serengeti.
- The unique bouncing and jumping of the fleeing gazelle are called "pronking" or "stotting".
- Thomson's gazelles calve twice a year and hide their young in the open fields, in tall grasses, just like deer.

- This gazelle was named after the Scottish explorer, Joseph Thomson, who explored Africa in 1890.

# Topi

- A topi is a medium-sized antelope with a striking reddish-brown to purplish-red coat. It looks like a cross between cattle and a deer.
- Their legs are yellow-tan in color that, combined with the bands of black, making topi's look like they are wearing stockings.
- The topi is territorial, and the males will mark their territories with piles of dung.
- The topi is a very social animal and lives in herds with a dominant male in the middle and young males

# Warthog

- Warthogs sleep underground at night in abandoned burrows that they steal from other animals such as the aardvark.
- Warthogs have short necks, when grazing they go down onto bent forelegs (like knees, but actually the wrist).
- Although warthogs look intimidating with their tusks, they actually only eat plants and like to graze for food.
- The fur on the backs of their neck acts like a mane of a horse and will stand straight up when the animals sense danger.
- Baby warthogs are called piglets. Mom's usually have litters of 2 or 3 piglets but may have up to eight.
- Warthogs can run as fast as 30 miles (48 kilometers) an hour.

- Warthogs are very social animals and can be found in groups of up to 40 warthogs.
- Warthogs don't really have warts; they are growths of thick skin meant to protect their face against teeth and claws of predators or aggressive males.
- Like pigs, warthogs don't have sweat glands to cool themselves.
- Warthogs are passive animals and are only aggressive when they feel threatened.

# Wildebeest

- Wildebeests are also called "gnus", (pronounced as either "new" or "g-new")
- Wildebeest follow the rains across Tanzania and Kenya, covering a distance between 500 to 1,000 miles each year, which is about one-third the distance from Los Angeles to New York.
- The wildebeest is a member of the antelope family.
- Calves can run with their mothers within minutes of being born and can reach speeds up to 40 mph.
- Blue Wildebeest got the name as their coat has a blue sheen.
- The wildebeest is a large antelope measuring between 45 and 55 inches at the shoulder and weighing between 300 and 600 pounds.

- Around 80–90 percent of blue wildebeest calves are born within two to three weeks of each other.
- Wildebeest and zebra graze together without competing for food. The zebras like to eat the longer grasses while the wildebeest like to eat the shorter grasses down low.
- Wildebeests have a better sense of hearing, while Zebras can see very well. Zebras have a great memory which helps them recall safe migration routes and make for great travel partners for the wildebeest.

## Conclusion

There you have it! A very comprehensive list of animals that are commonly seen in East Africa and the Serengeti National Park. I hope you have enjoyed the fun facts and even learned something that you didn't know before.

As independent publishers, we rely on reviews to help us get noticed. If you enjoyed this book and learned something new then I ask that you pay it forward and leave a review so that others may find this book. I'd like to know what fact you thought was the oddest or the most unusual!

All the best,

Lori Benson

**Index**

| | |
|---|---|
| Aardwolf | 5 |
| African Buffalo | 6 |
| African Elephant | 8 |
| Baboon | 10 |
| Bat Eared Fox | 12 |
| Bat faced Vervet monkey | 13 |
| Burchell's Zebra | 14 |
| Cheetah | 16 |
| Crocodile (Nile Crocodile) | 18 |
| Dwarf Mongoose | 20 |
| Eland | 21 |
| Giraffe | 22 |
| Grant's Gazelle | 24 |
| Grey Crowned Crane | 26 |
| Hartebeest (Coke's Hartebeest) | 27 |
| Hippopotamus | 28 |
| Hyena | 30 |
| Impala | 32 |

| | |
|---|---|
| Kirk's Dik Dik . . . . . . . . . . . . . . . . | 34 |
| Kori Bustard . . . . . . . . . . . . . . . . . . | 35 |
| Leopard . . . . . . . . . . . . . . . . . . . . . | 36 |
| Leopard tortoise . . . . . . . . . . . . . . | 38 |
| Lion . . . . . . . . . . . . . . . . . . . . . . . | 39 |
| Marabou Stork . . . . . . . . . . . . . . . | 41 |
| Ostrich . . . . . . . . . . . . . . . . . . . . . | 42 |
| Rhinoceros . . . . . . . . . . . . . . . . . . | 44 |
| Rock Hyrax . . . . . . . . . . . . . . . . . . | 45 |
| Secretary Bird . . . . . . . . . . . . . . . | 46 |
| Southern Ground Hornbill . . . . . . . | 48 |
| Superb Starling . . . . . . . . . . . . . . . | 49 |
| Tawny eagle . . . . . . . . . . . . . . . . . | 50 |
| Termites . . . . . . . . . . . . . . . . . . . . | 51 |
| Thomson's Gazelle . . . . . . . . . . . . | 53 |
| Topi . . . . . . . . . . . . . . . . . . . . . . . | 55 |
| Warthog . . . . . . . . . . . . . . . . . . . . | 56 |
| Wildebeest . . . . . . . . . . . . . . . . . . | 58 |

Printed in Great Britain
by Amazon